Two
Hats

One family's month-long
experiment in spending, giving
and generosity.

The Unedited Journal of Joel Holm

ISBN: 9780986181917
ISBN-13: 978-0-9861819-1-7

DEDICATION

To everyone who has ever wondered how much is enough.

ACKNOWLEDGMENTS

Thanks to my family, Marie, Rachel, Josh and Lisa, without whom Two Hats would have never been a reality.

Introduction

I sat down this morning for my Bible reading. I am reading the life of Jesus through the gospels. Today's passage was from Luke 3. John the Baptist is baptizing people. He tells them, "You've chosen a new way to live, so now act it. Be fruitful. Show the results from your new way of living." The people in turn ask him, "What are we supposed to do?" He responds, "If you have two hats give one away to someone who has none. " He doesn't say "Find the hat you haven't used in 5 years that is old and hanging alongside the ten other hats you own." He tells them for every item you own give another one away. I can't stop thinking about this. This is not how I live my life. This is when God gave me an idea, a spiritual experiment. For every dollar our family spends in the month of December – no matter what it may be for - we will give the same amount away. If we spend $100 on groceries we will buy another $100 worth of groceries and find someone to give it to.

Each day I will record my spending and giving and journal any lessons I learn for that day. There are a few guidelines I have created for this exercise:

I won't monitor the income. The purpose is not to learn about His provision. I believe in a God who provides, blesses and rewards but I have a conviction that the income side of this month has little bearing on what He wants to teach me.

I will match our giving to the same type of spending. If we spend money on the house, we will provide for housing. Food for food. Clothes for clothes. I will stick to the idea of two hats, not a hat and a coat, and see what connections God makes.

I am a firm believer that Christ followers should give 10% of their income to their local church as an act of worship to God. This experiment will in no way alter that.

Joel Holm

December 1

I am not a saint. I am not a martyr. And I do not think I am a fool. I am just a normal person who – like those baptized by John the Baptist – is a follower of God, trying to figure out what that exactly means. I have faith and I get scared at times. I love God and I don't always love others, including myself. I give and I covet. I am just a normal person, trying to do something for one month that is a bit abnormal, hoping it makes my life far less average.

Today is Dec. 1. Having spent the day determining whether or not this idea is from God, it is now the end of the day. There is no real activity to report except feeling a bit ridiculous. I am glad no one knows I am doing this besides my family and one friend that I have asked to help me process this. Tomorrow the adventure begins I suppose.

December 2

Today was the first day of this month-long exercise. I woke up eager to get started. I almost wanted to go out and spend money just to see how it would work to then have to give the same amount away. I'm guessing that kind of passion won't be present for the whole month.

Today I spent $75 on air filters for our furnace and Christmas lights so I put $75 in an account to give to Pastor Regina for housing teens in the Kenyan slums. We get Christmas lights and the teenagers in Africa get clean water. Seems like a weird trade off.

We had an interesting moment when Marie took Lisa to get her haircut. Marie asked the hair stylist if she knew someone who couldn't afford a haircut. Again, "two hats" means I try to match our giving with our expense. Marie didn't go into all the details regarding our month-long experiment. She simply told her we were interested in sponsoring someone to have her hair cut. With great surprise the hair stylist told Marie of a lady who has been a client of hers for many years but whose business just went bankrupt. This lady is incredibly depressed. We paid for her haircut. The hairstylist will call her today to set it up.

I wonder if a haircut paid for by an unknown stranger can inspire someone and lead her to Christ? I wonder what the hair stylist thought of all this.

The most fascinating aspect of today was watching my 15 year-old daughter listen with interest as the connections for our experiment - the hairstylist and the lady who's business went bankrupt - all came together. I thought of all the conversations and actions my daughter has witnessed in my life. How many were about what we could get and how many were about what we could give?

December 3

I visited a Christian bookstore today where I casually purchased $80 worth of books. It was 11 am and I had already forgotten about my Two Hats experiment. I was just going about my daily activities as I have for years.

As I was walking away from the bookstore, it hit me like when you remember that you forget your wallet while standing in front of the cashier. I remembered that I now had to buy $80 worth of books for someone else. I'll get these for my friend who leads a ministry in India who otherwise would never have access to these kinds of books.

Two things happened today that I didn't expect:

First, I forgot very quickly about the exercise. It took almost no time for me to lose focus of my spending and giving.

Second, my first thought upon remembering I had to buy another $80 worth of books was 'Rats!" But almost immediately that changed to "Wow – what should I buy?" It became exciting as if I had been given permission to spend money I otherwise would not have been able to. I went from "I have to give up my money" to "I get to share God's money" in a nano-second.

Interesting that because the giving this month is out of my control (it's a command from God to do the experiment), I find a freedom and joy in being able to give to others. What commands about money in the Bible have I been considering only as recommendations? And does that stop me from being more free to share?

I wonder what Marie spent today?

December 4

This morning I had a meeting at Starbucks. I love Starbucks. I'm not sure if that makes me a bad person; or a superficial person; or someone uncaring about a farmer in the hills of Bolivia; but I like getting a Starbucks coffee.

I spent $4 on a triple Grande wet cappuccino and $2 on an old fashioned donut. Just like yesterday it wasn't until later that I considered what I had spent. Unlike yesterday, this time I thought about the fact that I had spent the equivalent of two days wages for many people throughout the world.

Is it right to get a positive spiritual vibe about buying books but to feel guilty about buying a coffee? Is God more interested in what I buy or in what I give? Its not like I haven't thought of these questions before, but it was definitely different this time. More vivid. More real, while I sipped my Starbucks coffee.

I didn't mind not having the answers. I was satisfied

with the clear questions that had come up from my Starbucks trip, but I am hoping this month is more than a discovery of questions.

Anyway, I put $6 into the food account that will go to buy groceries for a food pantry. I wonder if I should give the food pantry a gift certificate to Starbucks. I'd rather have that than a can of beans.

I subtly got my co-worker to buy me a second cup so I wouldn't have to give more money away. Not the best solution for watching your spending but I am definitely becoming aware of how I spend.

December 5

Today was a pretty uneventful day. Actually with only five days of living out this experiment, the thrill has already worn off. Today this experiment seemed like a lot of labor. Keeping track of every dollar spent by every person in a five person family is no easy task for me. Keeping track of this can be overwhelming. I'm not sure an hour goes by that I don't spend money on something.

Regardless of the amount, I wonder how many people in the world spend money even once a week? I wonder if the remaining 25 days will be more labor or intrigue? Then tonight this experiment got interesting again.

Tonight I started thinking about my dentist appointment on Monday. I need X-rays, which means the bill is going to be higher. We don't have dental insurance so I have to pay the cost directly, which also means I have to match those funds. What made this evening interesting in some bizarre way was thinking how I would make a connection between my mouth and sharing with someone else. Was God going to have me come across someone with bad teeth? I've never thought about other people's teeth before. I bet a mom having a child with a cleft lip and no money for surgery, thinks about this everyday.

December 6

For the past five days I have been writing my journal at the end of each day. I am starting early today because I want to capture how I am feeling early this morning. I sat down to read the newspaper this morning. I hadn't really thought about the month-long experiment yet, until I turned to a classified ad section of the paper. I saw an ad for a not - for-profit organization that provides cleft lip surgeries for children who would otherwise never be able to afford one.

All of a sudden I remembered how yesterday I had been thinking about how I would ever connect my upcoming dentist appointment to a giving opportunity. I couldn't help but think that God had provided me a connection. Of course I could've done the research and found an organization that does these surgeries, but I have to tell you what an incredible sensation it was to see this ad 12 hours after having thought of the same idea.

Then I began to wonder: Have my eyes crossed over this ad many times before but I just never really noticed it?

Perhaps it has always been there but I never had the awareness to truly see it. Maybe the opportunities are not new - as much as God is giving me new eyes to see the opportunities that have always been right in front of me.

Today's Sunday – I imagine it will be a really good day of worship in church and then a depressing Sunday afternoon as the Bears (my sports team) lose.

It's now evening so I'm adding to today's entry: Sunday must be a day of rest for us because we finally lived through an entire day and didn't spend hardly any money. When I got gas, I didn't wince at the cost per gallon. I did think how the $32 I spent on gas could buy bicycles for a family in India that otherwise had to walk miles for water. I wish I had a monster truck and had to buy $800 worth of gas - then I'd be forced to buy more bikes for India.

December 7

We spent $361 on food and groceries in one week. Our cupboards are full and tonight we went out to buy food for the Food Pantry in town. We split up into two teams of shoppers: Josh and Lisa (two of my kids) on one team and Marie and I on the other. Buying the food didn't take long at all, no more than 20 minutes.

I found myself praying for whoever would be eating this food. I wonder what their lives are like? I am glad they don't know who I am because I think I'd be embarrassed that I have done so little to help my neighbors until now.

Today we bought a cleft-lip surgery for a child. The cost of the surgery was equal to two regular visits to the dentist. Two of us in our family have clean teeth today. One child in South America will have her life transformed. It makes me shake my head in bewilderment. It makes me really angry, mainly at myself. It's easy to blame an unjust global distribution system that allows my family to have regular cleanings and another family to live with the pain of a child with no options.

But I am the global distribution system. This is my responsibility.

I continue to be confronted with the radical imbalance of life. It shouldn't be but it is. And I feel helpless to do anything about it. I want to Google and see how many cleft palette kids exist in the world but it would just depress me. I don't have enough teeth in my mouth to get cleaned.

December 8

This morning I dropped off the groceries we bought last night for the Food Pantry. There was a long line of people waiting to get into the building to receive their food. Some looked like they really needed help. Others I have to admit, didn't look like they needed free food. One drove up in a car a lot nicer than mine.

But then I wondered why the status of these people would be the first thing on my mind. Why would I wonder that? Do people need to "qualify" in order to be eligible for free food?

I hated dropping the food off while everyone was standing in line. I had to carry bags of groceries past them, with each looking at me. The last thing I felt like was any type of hero or saint. I don't know what it feels like for them. I know it was embarrassing for me. I read that the poor don't see themselves the way others do. For them, being poor is a reflection of their identity, their value.

I wondered if walking past them with the food

handouts only reinforced a mindset that marginalizes them and holds them back.

I delivered hundreds of dollars of food to a food pantry desperately in need of stocking its shelves for people that would be grateful - and yet I didn't have any sense of feeling good about what I'd done. That can't be healthy.

December 9

I thought I'd make it through the whole day without spending a dime. No such luck though. Today I bought a book for Lisa that cost me $16. The book is called Three Cups of Tea. It's the story of a man who builds schools for children in Afghanistan and Pakistan. Lisa, my 15 year-old daughter is working to build a school for kids in a village in the tea plantations of north India. Sounds crazy huh? Maybe there's a bug going around our family. Who's next?

Then again maybe all of us need to live each day a lot crazier than we do! Honestly, what do I have to lose? What do I have to gain? So far, a great deal of mixed up thoughts, emotions and battles.

Today I was consumed with the hope that there would be one day in the month of December when I wouldn't spend any money at all. And that it would happen in the natural flow of the day rather than having to lock my family in the house.

Am I strange? Does anyone live in a way where you can go for days and not spend money? Maybe farmers in Iowa.

December 10

Amazing! I lived through the entire day and didn't spend a penny and I wasn't locked inside of a room. Of course it was 28 degrees below zero outside.

I also lived through most of the day and didn't think about the rest of the world. I wonder if I will ever think about the world, without needing a reminder, like how much money I'm spending. I wonder if I'll ever think of the world, not because of my generosity or greed but just because of who they are.

Today marks the one-third way through this month-long experiment. Wow – the last thing this is, is an experiment. I'm not sure – after ten days – how I would label it. It's many things but more than anything, it's a window.

My life needs windows. Windows let me look in and out, depending on my viewpoint. I need to be able to see myself from another perspective. I need to see others from another perspective. I'm discovering windows need to be intentionally created, as my natural tendency is to live life only with mirrors.

Joel Holm

December 11

I wondered if a day like this would happen throughout the
month. It was a day of nothing. No lessons. No hardships.
No great divine intervention. I got nothing today. No
insights. No "aha" moments. Today was as average a day
as one could imagine.

It was just a normal day with regular routines. Maybe
sharing equally with others should be this normal. Maybe
today is supposed to be what most days should look like.
Lifestyle. Routine. Maybe I shouldn't need "aha"
moments and divine connections to inspire me.

What if today's lesson was to simply live a life that shares
fully and compassionately? Maybe following Christ is
about not being too impressed with myself as I live out a
normal day in God's Kingdom.

December 12

Twelve days into this exercise and it's getting harder
and harder. I find myself getting exhausted in trying
to match the giving to the spending we do. I need to
find more inspiration so that the rest of the month
doesn't become mundane. It's not just about giving
the same amount away. It's about matching our
giving with our spending. I am discovering it's far
more about who we give to, than how much we
give.

I am learning that with giving comes greater
responsibility. Responsibility to pray for and be aware of
those I am giving to. By giving to them, I feel like I am
also committing myself to them.

That is a new twist in this "experiment" for the rest of the
month. I need to commit to pray for those who are
receiving. For example, today I bought fifty $10 gifts cards
for families receiving food parcels at our church. We have
now committed to pray for these families, whose names
we don't even know. We need to pray and be aware of the

plight of students in the slums of Kenya who are getting housing through our experiment. We need to pray for the lady who got her hair styled. Whether in a small or large way, they have to continue to be a part of my life – after I give them something – at least through this month. Maybe that's the source of inspiration. It's not in the matching of funds but in the people who are being matched to me.

I'm praying for energy to find life and inspiration in this month and not just obediently go through the routine of giving. Giving should never be routine. It should be intentional, spontaneous, and even creative. Maybe that's the missing piece. I've always understood and measured giving in terms of faithfulness but rarely in terms of creativity. What I'm learning is how God is a Creative God, even when it come to giving.

December 13

I went to church. I couldn't help but wonder how many of the people receiving our money are in church somewhere today. I love church. I go to church. I want everyone to go to church. But aren't we supposed to be going to people as well?

My prayer on this Sunday is "Lord please help me see what I don't even know to look for. Help me to see with different eyes so I don't just see the poor and the hurting, but I see You in them."

Jesus said, "When you feed the poor and clothe the naked, you're feeding and clothing me." I think I'm bringing Jesus and His love to these people this month, but in reality they are bringing Jesus to me. I am discovering more of Jesus this month, through these people.

I don't want to waste a single opportunity and not see Jesus. This is my prayer today. Wow – what is it about Sundays? I even write more spiritually than on weekdays!

December 14

Our family got two more haircuts today. Four heads down, one to go. I can't wait for bald to become fashionable for old white guys. Anyway, my daughter came up with the idea that we should give the money to a charity that provides wigs for kids struggling with cancer. I went online to find an organization and got bombarded by an online debate regarding the legitimacy of this charity. Here is another big problem with giving.

People don't know who to trust. Are there too many questionable charities or are we too demanding in our giving? Maybe we have just become too skeptical because people are always trying to take advantage of us no matter what the reason.

The detachment, confusion and skepticism that comes with giving makes it a lot easier just not to get involved. But when you become a giver you are required to really engage because of how much corruption exists. That's why I do most of my giving to my local church. It is my community and my family. I can trust my church because I am a part of it.

I am learning that my giving is far more about my sense of responsibility than my sacrifice. God is asking me this month: What am I responsible for and how seriously am I taking that responsibility?

This month would be a lot easier if it was just about money.

December 15

Today I am halfway there. I never expected it to be this challenging. It takes a lot of energy just to keep track of the spending. I am not referring to just the numbers but always having the experiment on my mind. I am constantly thinking about how much I am spending and in what way I am spending. It is exhausting. I don't want to think about this everyday anymore.

I suppose having to think about how much I am spending is a choice most people in the world never get. They have to think about every dollar every day (just usually not in dollars). They don't have the luxury of forgetting how much they are spending, even for a moment.

I'm too tired to write anymore today.

December 16

We were going to go shopping for the food pantry tonight. Plans change however. We will go shopping for food tomorrow. Somehow I ended up at home alone tonight and decided to take the time and do a little research on buying food for people.

I discovered that there are options for how to go about buying food for people. I can buy and donate groceries to the pantry. That's good. Or instead of buying the food, I can donate money to the pantry and they can buy groceries at a greater discount than even Wal-Mart would give me. That's better. Or instead of buying food or donating money to the pantry, I can donate money to the greater food association that the food pantry is a member of. This association can purchase groceries at one fifth of what it costs me and has even greater buying power than the local food pantry itself.

I wonder why it is that people would rather buy the food and give it directly to the food pantry; and why the local food pantry would rather get money directly

and buy the food they need, when the association can
get it cheaper for them? And again, why the
association would rather get the money, buy the food
and give it to the food pantry? Everyone seems to
want to be in control of the purchasing power.

Is it most important to personalize my experience so I'm
the one to buy and give groceries away? Or should I find
the most cost effective way to give money so that more
people can be fed, even if it means I am more detached?

I thought about this through much of this evening and
came to the realization that ultimately my connection
needs to be with Christ, not just with financial efficiency
or even the people. When I give – whether its food
directly or money – I am giving to Christ. It is an act of
worship that He seems to give high value to.

December 17

Today our family went shopping to buy our Christmas dinner. Christmas dinners are always special. Today however, while we were shopping, Marie talked about feeling guilty over how much money we are spending on food for our Christmas dinner.

Things got a little tense. It's one thing when a month-long experiment challenges your giving. It's a whole other thing when you then add guilt to the emotional roller coaster ride of the month.

Guilt is neither good nor bad. It is either true or false. Question is: Does buying food for a special Christmas dinner warrant guilt? I have to find a way, as a middle class American, to live in grace. I have to be able to watch my spending, give generously, live happily and not live in guilt.

This is no easy task when everyday I am bombarded with contradicting positions. The world is poor and hungry while I live very nicely. I don't believe that I am supposed

to sell everything and live in a broken down Volkswagen
bus, but neither am I supposed to spend too much
money on myself.

I can't get away from the poverty of the world and the
affluence of my life. They are both present in my life
and they don't seem to get along very well.

I've heard more than my share of teachings; read books;
and had discussions with friends. Everyone experiences
this struggle. But no one has yet to give me a formula for
what is just the right amount to spend on a Christmas
dinner.

December 18

Today was a very cool day for this experiment. I cannot say this for everyday, but today I really liked participating in this experiment. This morning I prayed for Divine guidance in how I should give some of the money to others. I wanted more than just an option. I was hoping for a real "God" moment.

For the first time I am hoping God will somehow continue this experiment, even after the month is over. But what made this day most fun was how others are "catching the bug".

We spoke to my daughter's piano teacher about providing money for lessons to someone, as Marie had paid for Lisa's piano lessons today. Her response was incredible. She paused and then told us she wanted to pray seriously about which person she should offer the piano lessons to. I was really impressed. She didn't treat this moment lightly. She saw God in it even though she isn't aware of the full month-long experiment.

Today I got excited. Our piano teacher taught me a valuable lesson. What if spending became a spiritual devotion? What if giving was treated as much a spiritual discipline as praying?

What if we prayed before our spending just like we do before our daily meals?

December 19

Today was a day for Christmas shopping. Money is flying out of my wallet like it's in a tornado in Kansas! I wonder if the fact that it's hard to keep track of Christmas present buying means anything.

There is this strange paradox today: on one hand I struggle with knowing how much is right to spend on Christmas presents while on the other hand I am really grateful we can buy our kids nice presents.

We have friends who only make presents for each other. Yuck! We have others who spend thousands of dollars on presents for each other. Yikes! I wonder if every family feels like they have hit the perfect balance when none of us really have.

I wonder why God put the birth of His Son right in the middle of the Holidays. The Holidays can be such a distraction from His Birth. Seems to me February would have been a much better month to celebrate His Birth –

far away from "Santa and Seasons Greetings". Then I could buy Holiday gifts and not spend all my energy wondering if I found the balance between celebrating Christmas and celebrating Christ.

I am learning to keep others and the principle of love before me at all times – as the guide in my decision-making. Loving others is a better guide for handling money than trying to find a healthy balance in my life isolated from others.

December 20

I can't help but think that maybe this experiment is a simple, helpful technique for people. Find one area of your spending and match it to give to others who don't have the opportunity to buy like you do. Maybe it's the food you buy. Or what you spend on recreation and fun. Maybe for some it's just matching what you spend on lottery tickets, as long as you don't expect any divine favors.

I doubt anyone would repeat matching everything like I have this month. I don't even plan to repeat it. But as I look to January, how do I pick which area of spending is right for me to match with my giving? I don't think it matters what it is as long as you begin to think about your gain and not your loss.

This month I have learned that giving has a lot more to do with what I have and how I give it than what people need. I have discovered that the Bible says more about my giving than it does to what people need. I have learned that God wants me to be a generous giver even if no one is in need. Giving is about sharing and sharing starts with what I have. I need to be giving out of my abundance. It is not the old tenth hat, after I've purchased nine good ones. It is one of my two hats. Others should have what I have, if God is the ultimate Giver of everything. This month He has taught me that as the Ultimate Giver, God chooses to share all His stuff through me.

How might the world change if each person matched one area of spending to one area of giving to others?

December 21

I sent an email to my friend Ron today. Ron is a Nepali minister who lives in Northeast India. I wrote him asking for his help to distribute the "transportation" expenses I've accrued during the month. I've known Ron for years. We've stayed in each other's homes. We are more than friends. We are brothers. Yet it was weird emailing him.

My first draft of the email didn't tell him about the month-long experiment. I didn't want to come across like I was bragging so I only told him I wanted to give some funds to help someone with transportation – like buying a bicycle for a student. But after reading the email I knew it wasn't right. It would be obvious to Ron that I was hiding something. It would be too out of the norm for me to communicate this way with him. So I rewrote the email and briefly told him of my experiment. That draft was worse.

It was worse, not because I was feeling prideful in telling someone of what I was doing. It was worse because of the person (Ron) I was telling. Ron lives everyday trusting God to provide for him and his family because he invests everything he receives into helping others. My one-month experiment is Ron's daily life, everyday. Why did it take a special month-long experiment for me to learn lessons and live different from society, when people like Ron do it everyday?

Today, the contrast of my life to Ron's life confronted me with how far removed I remain from really giving to help others.

There is nothing heroic about this experiment or about me. The experiment is simply God's gracious way of taking an immature follower and nudging him one step towards a Christ-like love for others.

December 22

It's only midday but I have to write this down to capture my emotions. I was reviewing my finances this morning and realized that we as a family had spent about $500 on Christmas presents for ourselves. So I had $500 to give to a family for Christmas. I really wanted to give it locally, to a needy family.

This is when I discovered something horribly wrong.

I sat on my bed and started praying for the Lord to connect me – in a divine way – to a poor family that I could give $500 worth of Christmas presents to. Then it hit me. I actually don't know anyone locally who's poor. Here I was praying for a miracle that Jesus would have never prayed when he walked the earth. He knew poor people. They were his friends.

For me, they have been a cause. If I don't have a church or an organization to distribute the money through, it won't get distributed because I don't know one poor family in my neighborhood! They exist. Sometimes well hidden by society, but nonetheless they exist. My life just doesn't intersect with them. Jesus' did.

I shouldn't need divine revelation from God to give $500 to a poor family. I should know that family intimately. I should already be helping them and learning from them as they help me. This should be part of my lifestyle of relationship. Instead I need a miracle for God to point someone out to me.

In this instance needing to divinely hook up
with a poor family is actually a sad
commentary on my life in my own
community.

But the theme around Christmas is one of hope and grace, so I am grateful for this lesson and now I have to figure out how to change this. I wonder how many others like me help the poor but don't really know the poor.

December 23

Today we bought a lot of great food as over the next few days we have 14 family members visiting us to celebrate Christmas. I was happy to buy all this food. I love my family and I have always experienced great times around food and drink. I think if you are going to be lavish, food and drink with family may be the one place where God smiles because of the great love and laughter around the table.

Later today I drove to downtown Chicago to pick up my mom at the Greyhound bus station. I thought for sure, here is where I could divinely connect with someone less fortunate. I wonder if Jesus lived in America would he prefer to travel on the Greyhound rather than at the airport, just to be closer to people like those he hung out with in the first century?

Thoughts like that used to irritate me. I still think they're a bit naïve but I find them more intriguing now.

A huge snowstorm blew in while I was driving into

Chicago. I was an hour late to pick up my mom. By the time I got there, she was already waiting for me inside the station. Cars were lined up everywhere on the street. Traffic was miserable. I was late. There was no place to park. So I double parked outside, raced in, grabbed my mom's suitcase and arm and quickly shuffled her to the car. I had no time to notice anyone in the crowd of people.

It was a living example of how my daily life stops me from helping others. I dash in and dash out, not even recognizing there is a crowd. I cannot be available because I have no space in my life for them.

No more.…..not after this month.

December 24

BREAKTHROUGH! Somehow today was different. It's hard to describe. It was not one specific incident that changed it. Something is definitely different today but not because of any act I did. It's as if I woke up this morning with a different set of values. Maybe the month has finally caught up to me and the pieces are coming together. All I know is that today my perspective is different. It is accurate.

I went to our church's Christmas Eve service and looked down the aisle at my wife and three kids. I am amazed at how incredibly rich I am. I also realized how often I allow trivial pseudo wealth distract me from real riches. The real riches in my life are people. The greatest wealth I have is the opportunity to love and help these people.

But my breakthrough is not just in the act of helping people, but also in the change of my heart. I wonder if this change will stay? I think it will, if I keep acting on this change. The real question is can I help others as a lifestyle, not an experiment, to keep my heart in the right place. I know I can help myself as a lifestyle. I've done that for 46 years. But to help others I will need some kind of system – some structure – a bit easier than this month-long experiment but nonetheless some way that helps me live generously as a lifestyle.

The key to this system is the people. The very people in my life that I love are the people to join with me in loving others. Living generously is never to be done alone. It is to be done with others, together. My church is to play a key role in this for me.

December 25

I stayed home all day today. It was one of the few days this month where I did not spend any money. I did start reviewing and considering the main lessons God has taught me through this month. I only have six days left on this spiritual experiment. I feel like a marathon runner who sees the last mile before him. I am finding an extra burst of energy. I hope to find time during the next few days to reread my journal entries and distill them down to the top three or four lessons I have learned.

I couldn't help but think that today celebrates a day when God gave His Very Best! All month I have given an equal measure. But He gave all and He gave His Best (Jesus) for us at our very worst. That is something my experiment did not provide for me: I did not give my best to someone who is not worthy, grateful or concerned for me. All month I gave to grateful, needy people. It feels good to help someone who needs and deserves help. But all month I have not given to nasty people. This is what God did – while I was yet a sinner, He gave His Son to die for me.

I have not given to the drug dealer who is hungry. I have not given to the lazy man who refuses to work to feed his kids. I have not given to the unrepentant prisoner who committed horrible crimes.

God gave a full share to people who are guilty. I have to admit that I don't want that to be my experiment for next month – to give a full share of my life to evil people, loving them unconditionally to see them transformed. That may be more than I can tackle. But that is the bar Jesus sets for me at Christmas.

December 26

26 days ago I started a spiritual experiment. I have only got 5 days left – whew! I'm on vacation the next few days so I'll be spending a little bit of money and will match it. But I also want to take these final few days to review and make some sense of what God has taught me.

Ironically for all the humbling experiences, I don't think God's most important lesson for me is how greedy or materialistic I am. The first lesson I learned is that I am not that different from anyone else, whether they have one hat, two hats or ten hats. I have a hat, I give a hat and now we each have a hat. It's not rocket science. One is not the hero and the other the rescued. The world for the most part is made up of average people, hopefully, each with a hat. It's best defined by hats not by careers, countries and bank accounts.

Having "stuff" fools me into believing that I am different from others. Even if I don't think I am better, I still see myself as different. But when you measure me against others by hats, I am pretty much the same. I am human. So are others. We should live humanly. We should talk human. When I discover how similar I am to the poor family living a few blocks away, I should live closer to them like Jesus.

If giving is about hats then giving is not just for the wealthy. It is also for the poor. Most poor people have two hats. The month did remind me how rich I am and how not to waste wealth. But it also taught me how close I am to poor. How they are the "same kind of different" (you should read the book with that title) as me.

This month I learned how sharing is God's way of reminding us how the same we all are.

December 27

Today was a relaxing day. The Christmas rush is over and we spent most the day just hanging out around the house. We spent nothing today, probably only one of five days this month that has happened.

My second lesson this month was to be more generous with no strings attached. I gave a lot of money away this month. More than I ever would have planned. I wonder if I could continue this exercise indefinitely. Could I do this for a year and not just a month?

I don't know. But I do know I can give a lot more to others than I have been. This month has been a paradox. On one hand I need to be more personally engaged in my giving but on the other hand, I need to be more generous in my giving with no strings attached. Give simply for the sake of giving. Share with no expectation.

A few days ago we gave some money to a homeless man. Many would criticize this as wasteful. "He's just going to go buy alcohol with it." But what about giving with no conditions attached? God has blessed me often, knowing I would squander His blessing on something stupid and unnecessary. But He still gave to me.

I learned this month that when I give, I am to give unconditionally. I am giving it to those He loves so much. For when I give unconditionally I am not only giving as God gave, but I am giving to God.

December 28

Another calm day, except today Marie paid our insurance bill – which wasn't due until January 10th. She could've waited until after January and saved us hundreds of dollars!

Maybe I haven't learned my lesson fully yet.

This reflects another lesson from this month-long experiment. My initial response to Marie's paying the insurance bill was one of weakness. I was trying to manipulate the system for my own good. I wasn't strong. I was weak.

Ironically I read today in the Bible how the Kingdom is advancing "forcefully" and how forceful, strong men take the Kingdom. The passage described a part of this month's experiment. I needed (still do) to learn about advancing forcefully with my money. I cannot be timid, hesitant, fearful and nervous about sharing and giving away my stuff. Throughout this month I have learned to become forceful, intentional and even aggressive in giving to others.

I am discovering the freedom of throwing caution to the wind and being forceful in my giving. I know the Kingdom is advancing and I know beyond a doubt that I have advanced this month.

December 29

There are only two days left in this experiment. I am not sure how to bring this to closure. Should I be elated or relieved? Honestly, I am neither. I am a bit sad.

It has taken a lot of effort to fulfill this experiment. But I know that something genuinely significant has happened in my life: Something that may have begun this year but will continue on indefinitely. Nonetheless in two days, this month-long experiment will be over.

Now I am faced with the question of how to continue being aware of my spending and my sharing? How do I translate one very intense month into a lifetime? I am grateful that I did not go through this month and come out with pithy answers to issues that are not at all pithy.

I may not have all answers I want, but I have an incredible sense of stability. The experiment is coming to an end in two days. If you were to ask me to tell you the one main takeaway from this month, I am afraid it wouldn't be so profound.

I would only tell you that I do not want to return to handling money as I did a month ago. A month ago I was blindsided by God's idea. Now I am praying He will give me another one for next month.

December 30

In reflecting on this month, I am beginning to realize that although the experiment has to do with money, it has more to do with faith and obedience in the grey. A month ago I thought I heard God direct me to do this experiment, but honestly my sense of hearing was "grey".

Grey is how I describe most of my life that lacks the certainty of black and white. Life is far more about shades of grey than black and white certainty. Did I really hear God on November 30th? Maybe it was just too much pizza the night before. But maybe God was specifically leading me.

I don't think it matters.

What matters is that somehow I found the courage to take on this experiment. Too often I don't. This month I learned a lot. I survived an intense month financially. But more than anything, I have the experience of living outrageously for God in the grey.

I wonder how many times there has been that whisper in the grey of life that I have dismissed. Invite this person to church. Volunteer for this project. Give this amount. I wonder what I would have learned had I tried it each time. I wonder whose life I could have changed if I was more willing to live outrageously in the grey.

One of the most important lessons of this month had nothing to do with money. My resolution is to hear every whisper and if the message comes in grey, to try it nonetheless, trusting that grey is God's favorite tone to speak in.

December 31

Wow. Its finally done....or is it just starting......

I am so grateful for having done this experiment this month. I would have never imagined how much a month like this could change me.

As I write this it is about 2 am, January 1. As I start this year I do so with no New Year's Resolution. My New Year's resolution started a month ago on December 1, with my Two Hats experiment. There is something very cool about starting a New Year's resolution on December 1st.

Now that I don't have to give a hat away everyday, I can't help but wonder what the month of January will be for me.

I am the same person I was 30 days ago. I am not moving my family to the slums of India. I am not going to stop going to Starbucks. This month doesn't read like a Hollywood movie script of immediate radical transformation. Instead of changing me, it's as if something rich and marvelous has been added to me. I am praying I don't lose it. The only way I know to keep it is to keep giving that second hat away.

ABOUT THE AUTHOR

No one quite knows what Joel does. He teaches, consults and serves leaders of churches, businesses and civic organizations in their global work. His favorite and most challenging role is that of husband and dad. When he is not thinking, working and learning, Joel spends his time exploring the world, having traveled to 93 countries.

To contact Joel and access additional resources visit joelholm.com

www.ingramcontent.com/pod-product-compliance
Lightning Source LLC
Chambersburg PA
CBHW071932020426
42331CB00010B/2827